Gao Yaojie: Physician, Grandmother, And Whistleblower In China's Fight Against Hiv/aids

United States Congress Senate

GAO YAOJIE: PHYSICIAN, GRANDMOTHER, AND WHISTLEBLOWER IN CHINA'S FIGHT AGAINST HIV/AIDS

ROUNDTABLE

BEFORE THE

CONGRESSIONAL-EXECUTIVE COMMISSION ON CHINA

ONE HUNDRED ELEVENTH CONGRESS

FIRST SESSION

DECEMBER 3, 2009

Printed for the use of the Congressional-Executive Commission on China

Available via the World Wide Web: http://www.cecc.gov

U.S. GOVERNMENT PRINTING OFFICE

55–539 PDF   WASHINGTON : 2010

For sale by the Superintendent of Documents, U.S. Government Printing Office
Internet: bookstore.gpo.gov   Phone: toll free (866) 512–1800; DC area (202) 512–1800
Fax: (202) 512–2104   Mail: Stop IDCC, Washington, DC 20402–0001

CONTENTS

GAO YAOJIE: PHYSICIAN, GRANDMOTHER, AND WHISTLEBLOWER IN CHINA'S FIGHT AGAINST HIV/AIDS

THURSDAY, DECEMBER 3, 2009

Congressional-Executive
Commission on China,
Washington, DC.

The roundtable was convened, pursuant to notice, at 10:07 a.m., in room 628, Dirksen Senate Office Building, Charlotte Oldham-Moore, Staff Director, presiding.

Also present: Douglas Grob, Cochairman's Senior Staff Member; Abigail Story, Manager of Outreach and Special Projects; Kara Abramson, Advocacy Director; and Anna Brettell, Senior Advisor, Congressional-Executive Commission on China.

OPENING STATEMENT OF CHARLOTTE OLDHAM-MOORE, STAFF DIRECTOR, CONGRESSIONAL-EXECUTIVE COMMISSION ON CHINA

Ms. OLDHAM-MOORE. I think we're ready to begin.

Good morning. We are very honored at the CECC to be hosting Dr. Gao Yaojie this morning. Before we turn to the program, I just wanted to make some quick announcements. The first, for those of you who are new to the CECC, please visit our Web site, *www.cecc.gov.* You can sign up for our releases, daily bulletins, and newsletters.

Our senior researcher on public health, Abbey Story will frame our discussion for today.

Before I turn to Abbey, I want to recognize the exceptional people with us in the audience today. We have Dr. Wang, who has done extraordinary work on HIV/AIDS in Henan Province and has faced many of the difficult personal experiences that Dr. Gao has confronted. Thank you for your presence here today.

I also want to acknowledge Mr. Jin Zhong, who is here. He's the publisher of Dr. Gao's book. If you want more information about Dr. Gao's book, please talk to Mr. Jin Zhong afterward.

Abbey, please begin.

STATEMENT OF ABIGAIL STORY, MANAGER OF OUTREACH AND SPECIAL PROJECTS, CONGRESSIONAL-EXECUTIVE COMMISSION ON CHINA

Ms. STORY. On Tuesday, World AIDS Day, about 20 people took over the stage at a Red Cross event in Beijing to petition on behalf of their family members who had been infected with HIV through blood transfusions. They demanded not legal redress for injustice, not monetary retribution, not due punishment for the corrupt officials involved, but simply the treatment that their sick loved ones could not afford. These are just a handful of the countless numbers who have been brutally impacted by the HIV/AIDS epidemic in China.

In February 2009, the Ministry of Health announced that HIV/AIDS had become "the deadliest infectious disease in China." The Ministry of Health and U.N. AIDS have estimated the number of HIV infections in China to be between 560,000 and 920,000, and the number of AIDS patients to be between 97,000 and 112,000; however, several NGOs both inside and outside China have argued that actual numbers are much higher. Testing and surveillance techniques are limited and reporting of cases remains incomplete. Realistic figures are therefore difficult, if not impossible, to ascertain.

China's first officially reported case of AIDS was found in an Argentine traveler who died from the disease in a Beijing hospital in 1985. In 1989, 146 cases of HIV were reported in the injecting-drug-user community in Henan Province, but the disease was viewed as having been "contained."

In the early- to mid-1990s, impromptu blood and plasma donation stations, established by enterprising businessmen and government officials, began to emerge in rural areas. Medical procedures in these facilities were often unregulated, needles and tubing were re-used, blood from donors was mixed, and once plasma had been removed, it was re-injected into donors of the same blood type. Such practices resulted in the rapid spread of blood-borne diseases, including HIV.

Whistleblowers such as Dr. Gao Yaojie and Dr. Wang Shuping independently began to link an outbreak of HIV infections in several rural villages to these tainted blood and plasma collection centers. Entire villages had been affected and children had been orphaned as their parents died of AIDS. Yet when these doctors reported their findings, they were met with authorities' harassment, intimidation, and even physical beatings.

In 1996, Dr. Gao Yaojie launched an aggressive campaign of education, prevention, and treatment starting in Henan Province and spreading across China. But even with these efforts, and others, HIV/AIDS cases were rapidly on the rise. By 1998, HIV had spread to all 31 provincial-level jurisdictions in China and was in a phase of exponential growth. Government authorities, however, maintained a policy of denial toward the spread of the disease in China, preferring to call it a "limited" problem resulting from contact with the West. By 2005, China had an estimated 650,000 cases of HIV infections, according to a joint report by U.N. AIDS, the World Health Organization, and the PRC Ministry of Health.

Today, HIV/AIDS continues to spread in China and is especially, but not exclusively, linked to needle sharing among intravenous drug users, unsanitary medical practices in underground blood and plasma centers, unprotected sex among both heterosexuals and homosexuals, as well as in the commercial sex industry specifically—which has grown in recent years due in part to increased mobility of migrant workers. The spread of HIV/AIDS in China is also linked to the general stigma, fear, and discrimination that promote silence on the issue instead of raising awareness.

The exposure of the official cover-up of SARS in 2003 brought change in the Chinese Government's attitude toward HIV/AIDS. Lest their dirty laundry be aired again to the global community about covering up another infectious disease epidemic, authorities instead began to acknowledge that there was an HIV/AIDS problem in China and that they were going to proactively address it.

Then-Vice Premier and stand-in Minister of Health Madame Wu Yi announced that HIV/AIDS statistics were no longer considered a state secret, and admitted cover-up of HIV/AIDS cases at the local level. The number of central- and local-level specialized laws and regulations on HIV/AIDS has increased steadily since 2003, and the government has initiated public service campaigns, including education programs, testing and treatment programs, free condom programs, and free single-use needle programs. These steps mark a progression from rejection to recognition of HIV/AIDS issues by the government.

With the increase in official attention to, and action on, the HIV/AIDS crisis has come increased crackdown on civil society efforts. Non-governmental organizations and individual activists play an invaluable role in HIV/AIDS education, prevention, and treatment in China, but they face ongoing government interference in many forms. Civil society organizations continue to be subject to strict registration requirements that limit their ability to legally function independently from the government.

Individual HIV/AIDS activists also continue to face serious obstacles in their work, including arbitrary detention, harassment, surveillance, intimidation, restrictions on travel, and other violations of their fundamental human rights. One such HIV/AIDS advocate, Hu Jia, is in prison today, serving a three-and-a-half-year sentence for inciting subversion of state power. His wife and daughter are under constant surveillance and are often prohibited from leaving their home.

We are honored today to have with us Dr. Gao Yaojie, who, despite enduring similar pressure, continues to fight for the cause of HIV/AIDS prevention, education, and treatment in China.

I will now turn over the floor to Charlotte to introduce Dr. Gao.

Ms. OLDHAM-MOORE. Dr. Gao Yaojie is a renowned gynecologist who sounded the alarm on a growing HIV/AIDS epidemic tied to contaminated blood banks in Henan Province in the late 1990s. In 1996, she launched a vigorous AIDS education, prevention, and treatment campaign, relying on her own personal funds and awards proceeds to support her work.

Despite authorities' continued harassment, intimidation, and limits on her personal freedom, Dr. Gao has visited several hundred villages in over 10 provinces, treated over 1,000 people, worked extensively with AIDS orphans, printed over 1 million copies of HIV prevention pamphlets and newsletters, and self-published her own book, "Prevention of AIDS and Sexually-Transmitted Diseases."

Dr. Gao has received an extraordinary array of awards for her work on HIV/AIDS issues, including the Jonathan Mann Award for Health and Human Rights, the government-run Central China Television (CCTV) "Ten People Who Touched China in 2003" award, as well as the "Vital Voices Global Leadership" Award.

Dr. Gao's autobiography, "The Soul of Dr. Gao Yaojie," was published in Chinese in July 2008 by the Mirror Publishing Company in Hong Kong. An updated version of her book, "China's AIDS Plague: 10,000 Letters" was released on December 1, 2009. Okay. Thank you, Dr. Gao. Please begin.

STATEMENT OF GAO YAOJIE, PHYSICIAN, GRANDMOTHER, AND WHISTLEBLOWER IN CHINA'S FIGHT AGAINST HIV/AIDS

Dr. GAO [via translator, Mr. Bob Fu]. Good morning, ladies and gentlemen. Today I would like to introduce to you some true situations about the AIDS epidemic in China. Actually, the first report about AIDS came out in 1982, and then in 1984 Professor Zeng Yi, an academic with the China Academy of Sciences in Beijing, reported blood contamination by the AIDS virus in the blood banks of some hospitals. But Mr. Zeng Yi told me, since he was working under government control, he could not report directly so I was encouraged to report first.

Then in 1988, the AIDS epidemic was reported and spread in Hebei Province first, and then in 1995, Dr. Wang Shuping first reported about this epidemic and her discovery of the tainted blood. I started my AIDS activist work from 1996, so this is the 13th year of my work.

For the sake of time, I will ask my translator to read a portion of my testimony.

Mr. FU. Dr. Gao's written testimony, you have a copy already. She has a few places she wants to emphasize.

Number one, the blood disaster and AIDS are national disasters. At present, the AIDS epidemic is rising in China. If you step in a village into an AIDS epidemic area, you will see newly-built, but vacant, houses. The neighbors will tell you that the house's owner built it with money earned by selling blood. Now the owner has died of AIDS and many new tombs have emerged in the fields.

According to an official report, the number of people infected with AIDS has grown by about 30 percent annually. For instance, from the following reports you can tell: from China Philanthropy Times in Heilongjiang Province, they reported on November 30, 2005; and Chinese Business Morning Review in Jilin Province reported on December 5, 2005; and Chinese Business Review in Liaoning Province reported on December 1, 2005; and North News reported on November 30, 2005; and Lanzhou Morning Post in Gansu Province reported on November 30, 2005.

In the 1990s, blood stations emerged like mushrooms after the rain. AIDS, a disease never heard of 20 years ago, is now spreading to all 31 provinces on the mainland of China. You may have heard that Henan Province is the highest prevalence area for, and the birthplace of, AIDS, but that is not true. AIDS is spreading even more seriously in other provinces, such as Shanxi, Shaanxi, Shandong, Anhui, Hebei, Hunan, Guangdong, Guangxi, Yunnan, Guizhou, Sichuan, and the three northeast provinces.

You may know Wenlou village in Henan Province, a famous AIDS village, but it is only one typical example of AIDS villages and a template set by the government. Who knows how many

AIDS villages like Wenlou there are in the whole country? How many of them can be treated in the same way Wenlou is treated? The spread of AIDS in China is staggering.

According to official figures, in 2006, China had 840,000 AIDS patients. Only 5 percent of the AIDS virus carriers can be located and the other 95 percent have merged into the population. Since 1992, the contaminated blood has flown to the whole country, from Shanghai in the east, to Urumqi in the west, from Heilongjiang in the north, to Guangzhou and Hainan in the south.

"Blood-mongers" sell large volumes of contaminated blood to bio-pharmaceutical companies in Shanghai, Wuhan, and other places to produce a series of nutritional medicines, such as albumin, globulin, interferon, and blood platelet components. These medicines have been sold throughout the whole country.

In the 1990s, the whole country was under a cash rush. The head of the Health Department in Henan Province proposed a new idea for earning money: encouraging the establishment of blood stations by all. The idea was called a "money-earning policy depending on seals internally and blood externally." They depended on official seals to issue certificates and collect money. They encouraged the local health departments and blood-mongers to organize farmers to sell blood. Apart from the blood stations run by health departments, many others were established by various enterprises, associations, and military units. In the early to mid-1990s, there were over 270 official and "legal" blood stations and countless illegal ones in Henan alone.

The official blood stations have been the most active advocates for the "blood economy." In those years, eye-catching posters saying "Honor to Blood Donors: Healing the Wounded and Rescuing the Dying" were common on the walls of hospitals in Henan. Blood-mongers told blood sellers, "Blood is like water in the well. It remains at the same amount no matter how much you have donated. Blood donation is like substituting old blood with new blood. It is good for the metabolism. Blood donors won't suffer from high blood pressure. Your body will benefit from it."

Disaster befell during the devilish back-transfusion. In addition, there were many deadly loopholes in the entire process. First, after blood extraction, both the disinfected scissors for cutting the blood transfusion tube and the disinfected clamp for clotting the blood bag would contact the freshly-extracted blood.

The separating centrifuge used then had 12 containers inside it, and each would accommodate two bags of blood. It was easy for the blood bag to be damaged during the separation. If the operator of the blood station operated casually and failed to discard the damaged blood bag, the red blood cells contaminated by the blood of other people would be transfused back into the body of the blood seller. If one of the blood sellers had AIDS or hepatitis, other blood sellers would all be infected.

Since 1999, many people have died of a "strange disease" in many places in Henan, including Dongguan village of Suixian County of Shangqiu, Shangcai County of Zhumadian, Wenlou village, and Donghu village of Xincai County, and Qulou Village of Weishi County of Kaifeng. People did not know that the perpetrator was AIDS until too many people had died.

When the fact that all these people were blood sellers was made known, the public began to understand the source of the disaster to be blood selling.

By October 2004, 12 people had died in the infamous Wenlou village, Shangcai County, Henan Province. Once, during a period of 10 days, eight people died.

In the same year, 34 people died of AIDS in the neighboring Houyang village, with the oldest aged 54 and the youngest 29, and either sex making up half of the death toll. In eight families, three generations were infected with AIDS and one family went extinct. In one family, 10 members were infected with AIDS, being the most amount of all infected families. Six members of this family have died, three in 2004. A pair of brothers died of AIDS within the shortest interval of 100 days.

Dongguan village of Suixian County had over 700 people, and half of them sold blood in those days. Among these blood sellers, over 100 were infected with the AIDS virus and some of them, mostly young and middle-aged, had shown symptoms. Before they were aware of AIDS, many people had died and their symptoms were quite similar to that of AIDS patients. Nobody could recall the exact death toll.

At this moment, the officials used their trump card: classifying AIDS as "secret" and stifling media disclosure of the truth. In fact, over a dozen reporters were dismissed and expelled by Henan Province. Outsiders were prohibited from visiting the AIDS villages, no matter what their intentions were, investigating truth or helping AIDS patients and orphans. Those who dared speak out were punished.

In this way, the truth about the AIDS epidemic in China has been covered up. Even today, after more than two decades, the truth about AIDS in mainland China is still unavailable. Many people at home and abroad only know that there are AIDS patients in Wenlou village, Shangcai County, Henan Province. What they do not know is that there are many unknown AIDS epidemic areas in China.

According to the latest official data, China had over 1 million AIDS virus carriers. Wang Longde, Vice Minister of the Ministry of Health, said on November 7, 2005, that "only 5 percent of the carriers could be located and the other 95 percent had merged into the population."

Blood trading is rampant in China. Many farmers sell blood from place to place. They may be in Henan or Hebei today, and in Shanxi or Shaanxi tomorrow, and in Shandong or Anhui the day after that. Each of the mobile blood sellers hold three to five "blood donor certificates" and they are professional blood sellers. These are reported in Fujian Daily, China Youth, Yangcheng Evening, Finance Magazine, and China Economic Times, and reporters from the China Economic Times carried out three rounds of investigation.

During a group consultation on April 7, 1996, I discovered a patient infected with AIDS due to a blood transfusion during a uterus operation. As she had received blood from a blood bank, my keen sense told me that she would not be the only one infected with the

AIDS virus this way. It was strange, however, that all of her family members, particularly her husband, did not catch AIDS.

After knowing my concern, an official from the provincial health department retorted, "You are good at making a scene. How can you be so lucky to see so many AIDS patients?" From then on, I began to doubt the past hearsay about AIDS spread by drug abuse and sexual promiscuity. Recently, I learned that, different from the situation in other countries, AIDS is spread in China mainly through "blood economy." However, government officials do not bear responsibility. They are using every trick possible to cover up the truth, safeguard their personal interests and the interests of their own group, and keep themselves in power. They have no concern about people's life and death. I had to investigate the spread of AIDS on my own.

I found many people infected with AIDS via blood or plasma transfusion. Take child patients, for example. They cannot take drugs or be engaged in sexual activity. Their parents or other close acquaintances showed negative results during HIV-antibody testing. They received blood from AIDS patients and they were totally innocent.

Seeing economic growth, the current government regards China as a harmonious society and a rising power in the world. However, what I saw in the countryside were poor people, badly in need of clothing and food. Violent cases happen from time to time in the whole country, and natural and man-made disasters occur one-by-one, especially the AIDS epidemic. AIDS will directly affect China's economic development and this is an undeniable fact. However, present-day Chinese have three characteristics: telling lies, practicing fraud, and faking.

In AIDS-related trade, there are numerous quacks—scam artists—and fake medical practitioners. There are now even fake patients. Chen Fengyao, a self-proclaimed businessman from Taiwan, has fooled people from northeast China to Henan. He spent 50,000 renminbi on hiring each fake AIDS patient to speak in his favor. He claimed to have cured over 300 AIDS patients.

I find what the Chinese authorities dread most is that the true situation of the AIDS epidemic will be made known to foreign leaders. When former U.S. President Clinton came to give a speech at Tsinghua University, I was invited to attend the AIDS and SARS International Seminar held on November 10, 2003, and asked to give a speech in the afternoon. I arrived in Beijing on November 7 and settled in at "Tsinghua Unisplendour International Center" at about 2 o'clock p.m. on November 9.

At 5 o'clock p.m., Shi Ji, Party secretary of my unit in charge of personnel, and Zhu Jinpin, chief of the old cadre department, suddenly entered my room and said that they came to see me. Giving them no more chance to speak, I left my room and went to Beijing Normal University with the head of the Law Institute of Beijing Normal University. Before I left, they asked when I would be coming back. I said "in the evening." That night I stayed at the Beijing Normal University and did not return to the hotel. At 8 o'clock a.m. the next morning when I was to enter the meeting room, both Shi and Zhu were waiting for me at the entrance. They said, "Do not mistake us, we just want to have a word with you." I said, "That is unnecessary. I will attend this meeting. When I come back, it is up to you to take whatever measures you like." Then a staff member of Tsinghua University's meeting organizing committee urged me to enter the meeting room. Shi and Zhu wanted to enter the room, too, but were stopped by the meeting organizing committee.

In the afternoon, foreign media made public the incident and asked, "Who said Gao Yaojie had personal freedom?" On November 12, I returned to Zhengzhou. Now, six years have passed and no leader has ever talked to me about this incident.

In 2007, the United States awarded me the "Vital Voices" Award, but the authorities obstructed my going to the United States and put me under house arrest for half a month. Thanks to the efforts of Mrs. Hillary Clinton, China finally let me go, however, they asked me to establish a foundation in the name of Gao Yaojie upon my arrival in the United States. I refused to do so. I was still under surveillance even in the United States and they blocked my information channels, which angered Zeng Jinyan, the wife of Hu Jia, to the point of tears.

After staying in the United States for over a month, many friends asked me to settle down in the United States. They said, "For your safety, do not go back." My career was in China and there are many AIDS patients and orphans who needed me badly. I could not bear leaving them, so I returned.

In February 2009, the U.S. Secretary of State Hillary Clinton visited China and requested to see me on February 22. The authorities agreed, ostensibly. I arrived in Beijing on February 19, and the following day they dispatched Zhao Fenli, a long-retired Vice Party Committee Secretary of TCM College, to Beijing, too. They even used the police to try to stop me. Zhao thought I might stay at Zeng Jinyan's home, so the national security personnel blocked Zeng's front door, prohibiting anyone from going out or in. In fact, I did not stay in Zeng's home. After two days of futile searching, Zhao failed to find me. As for me, I was honored to be able to meet with the Secretary.

According to some relevant literature, the AIDS virus, or HIV, belongs to a human slow virus group within a slow virus genus in the reverse virus family. There are different gene types and biological types and molecule types. In central China, most AIDS virus infection cases are caused by B-subtype virus, which is rarely spread via sexual activity.

Let me wrap it up.

Ms. OLDHAM-MOORE. Bob, do we have the complete testimony out front?

Mr. FU. Pardon me?

Ms. OLDHAM-MOORE. Do we have of the complete testimony out front?

Mr. FU. Yes.

Ms. OLDHAM-MOORE. Great. Okay. Good.

Mr. FU. Yes.

Let me finish this that she wants to emphasize. At the end of March 2009, a lady in the French Embassy called me: "France has decided to award you the 'Women's Human Rights' Award."

On the morning of May 6, my telephone line was cut again by the authorities. At noon, a friend came to pick me up. She said,

"You'd better leave. Trouble comes again." We had no time for lunch and immediately took a bus to Beijing. Three days later, I went to Langfang city. Over half a month later, I went to Sichuan. In early June, I went to Guangzhou, and on June 12 I settled down in Minglang village, in the suburbs of Guangzhou, a quite remote area.

In the past three to four years, I have realized that the AIDS epidemic is still serious in rural areas and blood stations have turned underground. Now there is a plasma station in Sunjiawan of Yunxian county, Shiyan city, Hubei Province. The operators organized over 10,000 women from the mountainous areas to sell blood at 168 renminbi per 600 milliliters, a China Youth article reported on November 4, 2009. There are many more undisclosed blood stations. So long as nobody speaks out, the officials can make a fortune and keep their grip on power.

They have five methods to deal with those who speak out: (1) buying off with money—giving bribes, poverty relief, disaster compensations, and so on; (2) material temptation—presenting food, articles, furniture, electric appliances, even houses, automobiles, and so on; (3) giving honors—awards, promotions, Party membership, and so on; (4) showing severe looks—suppression, punishment, threatening, monitoring, house arrest, even making rumors, and so on; and (5) the last resort for those unyielding to the aforesaid methods: fabricating a charge to frame them and send them to re-education through labor, criminal detention, and even imprisonment.

These five methods are so effective, that many who have dared to speak out before have surrendered to temptation and threat. Some of them never speak out again. Some "able men" make an about-face turn and begin singing songs of praise: what a peaceful and prosperous society: AIDS is set under forceful control and the blood disaster is gone. They predict that in the future, AIDS will be spread mainly by drug abuse and sexual activity. Of course, the officials who have made a fortune by selling blood have also made excellent political achievements. Their personal interests and the interests of their group are maintained. No one cares about the well-being of the ordinary people.

Thank you.

Ms. OLDHAM-MOORE. Thank you, Bob Fu, for doing that great service for us.

Now we turn to questions from the audience for Dr. Gao. When you stand up, you've really got to project your voice because there's a fan in the background.

Does anybody have any questions for Dr. Gao? Yes. Hi. Please say who you are if you want to, and your professional affiliation.

AUDIENCE PARTICIPANT. [Off microphone].

Ms. OLDHAM-MOORE. For those who couldn't hear in the back, U.N. AIDS said last week that the main source of AIDS in China is sexual conduct, and I would think, intravenous drug use. Her question is, to Dr. Gao: what is your assessment on the main causes?

Dr. GAO. [Responded in Chinese.]

Ms. OLDHAM-MOORE. She's giving you, I guess, a CD that will answer your question.

Mr. FU. She said: "The first case I found is through blood transfusion and many Chinese farmers sold blood and got infected. So, I have these CDs with many photos showing these facts. They are the results of my investigation."

Ms. OLDHAM-MOORE. Okay. Thank you. Did that address it?

Dr. GAO [via translator, Mr. Bob Fu]. The blood donation, the blood transfusion, and the blood selling has never stopped. So even in January 2008, I met with 58 AIDS-infected patients who were infected through the blood transfusion. Over 200 people rose to rebellion and tried to report about the truth about AIDS over 600 times and they were all suppressed by the government.

I do acknowledge the existence of those infected with AIDS through sexual activity, but only about 10 percent of them. According to Professor Gao, he surveyed and found, among 500 people, only about 50 people were infected through sexual activities. The type of AIDS virus is so radically different in China than in other foreign countries, and there are A, B, C, D, and E types of the AIDS virus. China belongs to the sub-B type and it's rarely transmitted through sexual activities or drug use. Among the first patients that I found, among his 10 family members, only 1 was infected. The rest of the nine had no AIDS. That one was infected through blood transfusion.

My next book is a conclusion of my 13 years of investigation and work. This little boy [shows picture] was born in 2004, but got a blood transfusion in 2005, and died in 2006, this lovely kid. He couldn't do prostitution or drug abuse; he was young, only a little over two years old. I don't want to get all my books published by one publisher because I could be accused by the government as collaborating for profit with one publisher.

Ms. OLDHAM-MOORE. Let's get another question from the audience. Is that okay?

Mr. FU. Yes.

Ms. OLDHAM-MOORE. Okay. Great.

Another question, please? Anybody? Yes, ma'am.

Ms. LEOPOLD. My name is Jennifer Leopold. I'm with RTI International, so we—implementing—largely around—HIV. My question is, why not ensure the blood supply? I don't understand what the motivation is for the government. If this is a financially lucrative business, the more community—the less they're going to give blood, so if you want to be competent and continue to build and sell blood, you would want to make sure that people are confident that it's a safe practice and continue the business as a lucrative entity. So I don't understand; maybe you can explain. What is the government motivation for not securing the blood supply?

Dr. GAO [via translator, Mr. Bob Fu]. Your question is very hard to answer because the government officials are busy selling and buying official positions and they got corrupted. So, they're so busy doing their business and they won't care about this. So, we have a different culture; don't use American measures to measure China.

Ms. OLDHAM-MOORE. Shellie Bressler, please.

Ms. BRESSLER. Hi. I am Shellie Bressler. I'm with the Senate Foreign Relations Committee and I handle HIV/AIDS issues for Senator Lugar. One of the questions my boss is very interested in is the AIDS orphans. In these villages where you've had a lot of family members die, who takes care of the AIDS orphans? Does the government take any responsibility to these children?

Ms. OLDHAM-MOORE. Bob, did you hear that?

Mr. FU. Yes.

Ms. OLDHAM-MOORE. Okay.

Mr. FU. Actually, Mr. To is here.

Ms. OLDHAM-MOORE. Oh.

Mr. FU. Yes. He's the foundation chairman.

Ms. OLDHAM-MOORE. Yes. Do you want him to speak to this? Is that what you're saying? He runs the AIDS Orphans Foundation.

Dr. TO. My name is Chung To. I work with the AIDS-impacted children in China. Just to answer quickly, the government has been building AIDS orphanages. That's where most of the children who are AIDS impacted stay. Sometimes they're taken care of by their grandparents or other relatives. The group that I work with, Chi Heng Foundation, has helped over 10,000 children impacted by AIDS in these villages. I'm—get resources—with other children in the villages. But there are other—who are also——

Ms. OLDHAM-MOORE. Sir, if you don't mind me asking, just to follow up a little bit on the question that was posed by the Henan Province project, what is your understanding or assessment of the failure to ensure the blood supplies?

Dr. TO. I think Dr. Gao's answer was most correct in saying that, although it may not be for the long-term benefit of the industry, when you're down to the local level, there are corrupt officials who are more interested in personal short-term gains rather than long-term development. I think we can see the same thing in—there might be long-term sustainability, but when you're down to the local level it's going to affect—corrupt officials who want to make some money to do things. So in principle, it might be down to the local level——

Mr. FU. So Dr. Gao also mentioned that of course the government wants to set up some model village with some orphans being taken care of, but when she and Mr. To traveled to those villages to find and look for these AIDS orphans, they were even chased and pursued by the government people.

Dr. GAO [via translator, Mr. Bob Fu]. There is another serious problem actually besides the AIDS orphans, which is the AIDS elderly, because the middle-aged died because of AIDS infection and they can't labor and work anymore, so nobody cares about them. So, it has become more serious now.

Ms. OLDHAM-MOORE. Kara Abramson, please.

Ms. ABRAMSON. I'm Kara Abramson with the Congressional-Executive Commission on China. Dr. Gao, I was wondering if you could talk about some of the challenges that HIV/AIDS patients who are not Han Chinese face inside of China. Are there specific efforts to address these communities? Are there adequate materials in languages other than Mandarin Chinese?

Dr. GAO [via translator, Mr. Bob Fu]. This is actually more terrible, the minority people who are infected, because they live primarily in remote areas and there's no transportation, no easy way to get there. The most serious thing is, they were charged, accused of being infected through immorality—sexual activity or drug use—

so they're ashamed and they don't want to tell the truth about the AIDS infection.

The most serious challenge is the fake doctors, fake medicine, and the use of fraudulent examples, like, they will pay 50,000 yuan to hire fake patients with AIDS, telling the world that they are healed by these medicines. Unfortunately, the government actually puts more resources toward dealing with people like me than handling those fake doctors and fake patients.

Like, somebody claimed that he was born from the eighth generation of Chinese medicine, a medical doctor, with expertise on healing AIDS. I said that's stupid because for eight generations, how long it would be, and how long AIDS has been in China. The other problem is, even some organizations claim they're rescuing and helping these orphans, but their main intention and purpose is to make financial gains.

Unfortunately, the government has paid no attention to dealing with them because they receive bribes by the corrupted officials. They even fooled the United Nations and the U.S. Embassy, these fake rescuers. They would pull a few children to dance on the streets saying that they were healed and being taken care of, and then people start donating money, and really it's for their own financial gain.

It's such an ugly situation, what these people did, that in the name of rescuing AIDS orphans, they're making their own gain, buying luxury houses. They are so despicable. Most of these so-called rescuers and helpers of these AIDS orphans are fake, and very few organizations are really helping. They are just making their own gains.

Ms. OLDHAM-MOORE. Except for him. He's the real deal.

Dr. GAO [via translator, Mr. Bob Fu]. One county Party secretary of Shangcai County, Henan Province, received $500 million yuan just out of this economy, the blood economy.

Ms. OLDHAM-MOORE. Okay. The next question. Abbey, do you want to——

Ms. STORY. I would like to ask a question that probably many in the audience are asking right now. In short, what can be done? I think we hear a lot of the negative, we hear about corruption on the local level, we hear about NGOs and foundations going in and doing the best they can, but being thwarted by the situation in that particular locality. I'm wondering, what do you, Dr. Gao, feel can be done to help this situation?

Dr. GAO [via translator, Mr. Bob Fu]. It's a social system problem. The question is a serious one, and it's hard for me to answer because it's a systematic problem, a political system problem, and because there are no officials without corruption in China.

When I was traveling to a village one time I saw one AIDS infected woman hang herself, with her little baby pulling her mom's leg. By the time I released the mom, she was already dead. It's so hard. Who can really solve this problem? I'm already 82 years old and I didn't see lots of hope in solving this. These are the three major issues in China: telling lies, making fake claims, and fooling people.

They are on all sides of the room with children. One Party official in Kaifeng city said, each child will receive 160 yuan for AIDS, and he would hold 100 yuan for himself. He said if anybody dared to report about this, they would receive zero support. So the only way I can answer your question is with my tears. So many people still, on all sides of China, did not know this truth. I'm already 83 years old.

There's no other reason for me to continue to stay in this world except to expose the truth with my books. I just want to awaken people in the outside, to know the truth, and to help them. Like, in this village when I visited there and saw both the mom and the child were infected, we have no other way to go but to just tell and leave behind the stories. That's very common in such a terrible situation.

The real problem is, those with the AIDS virus usually survive 10 to 20 years. Most affected are illiterate and uneducated and they are not able to speak up. So unlike the victims of the poisoned milk powder, these AIDS patients have a death rate 10 times greater than those that are infected by the poisoned milk, but who knows about them? They are now able to speak for themselves about this disease. Who has slept on a bed like this for all of you?

Ms. OLDHAM-MOORE. Anybody else? I think we'll wrap up in a few minutes. Does anybody else want to ask a question?

Yes. Doug Grob, please.

Mr. GROB. Doug Grob, Congressional-Executive Commission on China. I'm wondering to what extent problems with the HIV/AIDS epidemic in China exhibits variance along urban and rural lines. Many social and economic problems in China look very different in cities than they do in the countryside. Is protection of the blood supply and outreach to people living with HIV/AIDS, different in cities in some way, in some identifiable way, than it is in rural areas? Have you heard of any city or anyplace in China where programs have gotten some traction, made some progress in some way.

Dr. GAO [via translator, Mr. Bob Fu]. The government set up many examples of villages or stations, like Wenlou village. There patients were treated, they were shown to the world, they're doing a good job. But who cares about those who are unknown? Who cares about those in the remote areas? Just let them die. The so-called economic boom is only benefiting that very small minority group of people. How terrible for those in the majority, and many are still living in extreme poverty.

In January, I even received some photos showing just terrible poverty and people cannot sustain. At the same time, these government officials are busy selling official positions and getting financial gain. Even in Henan Province, the Party secretary recently was dismissed and was it was reported he was selling official ranks. Some officers were just busy promoting themselves, without really caring about anybody else.

These Chinese, these blood sellers, actually they were forced to sell the blood. They were in extreme poverty and they sold their blood in order to pay tuition for their children, they sold their blood in order to pay the fines for the family planning officials. They sold blood to buy fertilizer for their own land. But at the same time, those government officials that you meet when you go to China and see the skyscrapers and beautiful things and all their mistresses, what are they doing? They're just going to South Korea and spending the taxpayers' money, making cosmetic operations to make them look beautiful, like the deputy governor of Henan Province.

Ms. OLDHAM-MOORE. Wow.

Anna Brettell, please.

Ms. BRETTELL. I'm Anna Brettell with the Congressional-Executive Commission on China. I know that there are NGOs and foundations from several countries that work with and give grants to Chinese groups that focus on HIV/AIDS. Most of the Chinese "non-profit" groups are associated with the government, but there are some independent groups; there may be 300 to 400 groups in China now. Most international funding is given to government agencies and government-associated NGOs. However, the more independent NGOs can be more effective at reaching some populations in China than the government-associated groups and I am wondering if there are effective ways that international funding can be channeled to the more independent NGOs in China?

Mr. FU. So the foreign fund, right? Or China?

Dr. GAO. [Responded in Chinese.]

Ms. BRETTELL. Actually, not very much money gets down to the NGOs, so I was wondering why.

Dr. GAO [via translator, Mr. Bob Fu]. So it doesn't matter how much there is. The problem is, most of them are not doing the job. They're just busy making personal gains, buying houses for themselves. Even if you delivered some funding to the children, then they will get it back from the children for their own personal gains.

Ms. OLDHAM-MOORE. Okay.

Dr. GAO [via translator, Mr. Bob Fu]. There's no such thing as a real NGO in China. They're collaborating together. The reason Mr. To can survive is that he has three advantages. He's the descendent of Mr. Sun Yatsen, he's an American citizen, and he used to work on Wall Street. Otherwise, he could have been arrested many times already.

Ms. OLDHAM-MOORE. Okay.

Dr. GAO [via translator, Mr. Bob Fu]. So there's no such thing as civil society, or civil organizations in China, or independent. They're all government-run, GONGOs. Like the Women's Federation, they're supposed to be grassroots organizations, but they're all controlled by the government. So, they're just collaborating with the government. I was very sad when, in 2007 during my first trip to the United States, I was followed by the Chinese Government agents. Every night in my own room, they reported about my activities late at night. Fortunately, this time I'm not followed, so far, by the Chinese agents.

Ms. OLDHAM-MOORE. Thank you.

Did she want to make just some final comments? Then we need to close down.

Dr. GAO [via translator, Mr. Bob Fu]. Just, my final word is, don't just burn your money in China. Find an effective way to really help the people. My second point is, the main majority, the primary channel of the AIDS infection is still through blood transfusion. The government's main concern is to protect its own ruling interests, their own authoritative rule, while leaving many people suffering. So I myself really am still suffering like that.

My purpose for the rest of my life, even to leave today, is really just to expose this truth and what benefit there is for me to continue to live in this world. I cannot sustain myself, having difficult conditions physically. Thanks to Mr. Jin Zhong to hurry up and make the first book available. I'm still waiting for a publisher to publish the second and third book of mine. I just want to reveal this truth to the outside world before I die.

Ms. OLDHAM-MOORE. Thank you, Dr. Gao. Thank you, Abbey Story and Bob Fu. Dr. Gao, you certainly have awakened us. We are so grateful to have you here. No doubt you will accomplish in the next year what many of us can't in the entirety of our lives. So, thank you very much.

[Whereupon, at 11:36 a.m., the roundtable was concluded.]

APPENDIX

PREPARED STATEMENTS

———————

Congressional-Executive Commission on China Roundtable

10:00 am – 11:30 am on December 3, 2009

Dirksen Senate Office Building, room 628

Testimony: Dr. Gao Yaojie

Ladies and Gentlemen: Good morning.

Today, I'd like to introduce to you some true situations about the AIDS epidemic in China.

In 1984, Zeng Yi, an academician with the Chinese Academy of Sciences in Beijing, reported blood "contamination by AIDS virus" in the blood banks of some hospitals. In 1988, after his discovery of the AIDS virus in the stored blood, Mr. Sun Yongde, chief physician of the Epidemic Prevention Center of Hebei Province, called for action by the Health Department of Hebei Province, CPC Hebei Provincial Committee, and even the Ministry of Health, and some relevant departments under the State Council. However, the officials turned a deaf ear to these voices and did not take any action to control AIDS. Even worse, to get rich, they promoted "blood economy."

The AIDS virus knows no national boundary, race, sex, or age. Once infected, the victim suffers tremendously in mind and body. They stray, worry, wonder, feel helpless and isolated, sink into desperation, and finally vanish.

Seeing too many partings in life or death, one will be overwhelmed by strong feelings. Before leaving this world, AIDS patients have endless words of love, hatred, and complaints to tell. They do not want to die. Their cry for life and their family members' weeping will crush your heart and make you cry too. Why do they dare not identify themselves? The misleading propaganda has named AIDS a sex-related "dirty disease," and AIDS patients risk endless discrimination if they are identified. But the fact is, in China, AIDS has spread mainly via "blood disaster".

I. "Blood disaster" and "AIDS" are national disasters.

At present, the AIDS epidemic is rising in China. If you step in a village into an AIDS epidemic area, you will see newly-built but vacant houses. The neighbors will tell you that the house owner built it with the money earned by selling blood. Now, the owner has died of AIDS and many "new tombs" have emerged in the fields. According to an official report, the number of people infected with AIDS is growing by about 30% annually.

1. *China Philanthropy Times* **in Heilongjiang Province reported on November 30, 2005:** At 5:00 AM on October 1, 2004, Yang, a 29-year-old staff member of the Construction Farm of the Bei'an Branch of Heilongjiang Province Land-reclamation Bureau, died of AIDS. Yang's death unveiled an earth-shattering case—the staff hospital at the construction farm had illegally collected and supplied blood for a long period of time, resulting in the AIDS-related deaths of at least 19 innocent people.

2. *Chinese Business Morning View* **in Jilin Province reported on December 5, 2005:** One day in October 2004, Zhang Xixia, a busy farmer in Dehui City of Jilin Province, suddenly had a long-lasting fever. In September 2005, Zhang was diagnosed as suffering from a gastric ulcer. Zhang went to Beijing for treatment and during the preliminary test at Beijing 301 Hospital, the HIV antibody test showed "positive" reaction.

3. *Chinese Business View* **in Liaoning Province reported on December 1, 2005:** Since 2005, Liaoning Province had discovered 145 AIDS patients and people infected with AIDS virus, being the highest number

reported over the years. Seven AIDS patients were found in Shancun Village of Shanyang County and most of them were infected when they sold blood in Shanxi.

4. *North News* **reported on November 30, 2005:** Inner Mongolia discovered 132 AIDS patients and AIDS virus carriers who caught the disease mainly through the blood channel.

5. *Lanzhou Morning Post* **in Gansu Province reported on November 30, 2005:** Over 1,000 people in a small county in southeast Gansu, who were not drug users or sex workers or whoremongers, were forced to sell blood by poverty. Since that time, 12 of them had been confirmed infected with the AIDS virus.

In the 1990s, "blood stations" emerged like mushrooms after rain. AIDS, a disease never heard of 20 years ago, is now spreading to all the 31 provinces in mainland of China. You may have heard that Henan Province is the high prevalence area for, and the birthplace of, AIDS. But that is not true. AIDS spreading is even more seriously in other provinces, such as Shanxi, Shaanxi, Shandong, Anhui, Hebei, Hunan, Guangdong, Guangxi, Yunnan, Guizhou, Sichuan, and the three northeast provinces. You may know Wenlou Village in Henan Province, a famous AIDS village. But it is only one typical example of AIDS villages and a template set by the government. Who knows how many AIDS villages like "Wenlou" there are in the whole country? How many of them can be treated in the same way Wenlou is treated? The spread of AIDS in China is staggering. According to official figure in 2006, China had 840,000 AIDS patients. Only 5% of the AIDS virus carriers can be located and the other 95% have merged into the population. Since 1992, the contaminated blood has flown to the whole country: from Shanghai in the east to Urumqi in the west, from Heilongjiang in the north to Guangzhou and Hainan in the south. "Blood mongers" sell large volumes of contaminated blood to biopharmaceutical companies in Shanghai, Wuhan, and other places to produce series of nutrition medicines such as albumin, globulin, interferon, and blood platelet factor. These medicines have been sold throughout the whole country.

In the 1990s, several hundred thousand people sold blood to the illegal blood stations in Henan Province and they were infected with the AIDS virus. The true number of these people should be five times the official figure.

In the 1990s, the whole country was under a cash rush. The Head of the Health Department of Henan Province proposed a new idea for earning money: encouraging the establishment of blood stations by all. The idea was called a money-earning policy depending on "seals internally and blood externally." They depended on official seals to issue certificates and collect money. They encouraged local health departments and blood mongers to organize farmers to sell blood.

Apart from the blood stations run by health departments, many others were established by various enterprises, associations, and military units. In the early and mid-1990s, there were over 270 official and "legal" blood stations and countless illegal ones in Henan.

The official blood stations have been the most active advocates for "blood economy". In those years, eye-catching posters saying "honor to blood donors: healing the wounded and rescuing the dying" were common on the walls of hospitals in Henan. "Blood mongers" told blood sellers: "Blood is like water in the well. It remains at the same amount much no matter how much you have donated. Blood donation is like substituting old blood with new blood. It is good for metabolism. Blood donors won't suffer from high blood pressure. Your body will benefit from it."

At that time, blood stations adopted the "plasma collection" method: collecting blood from many people, mixing the blood together, separating the plasma and red blood cells with a centrifuge, selling the plasma to pharmaceutical companies, and transfusing the mixed red blood cells back into the blood sellers.

Disaster befell during the devilish back transfusion. In addition, there were many deadly loopholes in the entire process. First, after blood extraction, both the disinfected scissors for cutting the blood transfusion tube and the disinfected clamp for clutching the blood bag would contact the freshly extracted blood. The separating centrifuge used then had 12 containers inside it and each would accommodate two bags of blood. It was easy for the blood bag to be damaged during the separation. If the operator of the blood station operated casually and failed to discard the damaged blood bag, the red blood cell contaminated by the blood of other people would be transfused back into the body of the blood seller. If one of the blood sellers had AIDS or hepatitis, other blood sellers would all be infected.

Since 1999, many people have "died of a strange disease" in many places in Henan, including Dongguan Village of Suixian County of Shangqiu, Shangcai County of Zhumadian, Wenlou Village, Donghu Village of Xincai County, and Qulou Village of Weishi County of Kaifeng. People did not know that the perpetrator was AIDS until too many people had died. When the fact that all these people were blood sellers was made known, the public began to understand that the source of the disaster to be blood selling.

By October 2004, 12 people had died in the infamous Wenlou Village, Shangcai County, Zhumadian District, Henan Province. Once, during a period of ten days, eight people died. In the same year, 34 people died of AIDS in the neighboring Houyang Village, with the oldest aged 54 and the youngest 29, and either sex making up half of the death toll. In eight families, three generations were infected with AIDS and one family went extinct. In one family, ten members were infected with AIDS, being the most among all infected families. Six members of this family have died, three in 2004. A pair of brothers died of AIDS, within the shortest interval of 100 days.

Dongguan Village of Suixian County in Shangqiu District had over 700 people, and half of them sold blood in those days. Among these blood sellers, over 100 were infected with the AIDS virus and some of them, mostly young and middle-aged, had shown symptoms. Before they were aware of AIDS, many people had died and their symptoms were quite similar to that of AIDS patients. Nobody could recall the exact death toll.

At this moment, the officials used their trump card: classifying AIDS as "secret" and stifling media disclosure of the truth. In fact, over a dozen reporters were dismissed and expelled by Henan Province. Outsiders were prohibited from visiting the AIDS villages, no matter what their intentions were: investigating truth or helping AIDS patients and orphans. Those who dared speak out were punished.

In this way, the truth about the AIDS epidemic in China has been covered up. Even today, after more than two decades, the truth about AIDS in mainland China is still unavailable. Many people at home and abroad only know that there are AIDS patients in Wenlou Village, Shangcai County, Henan Province. What they do not know is that there are many, many unknown AIDS epidemic areas in China.

At 6 PM on November 22, 2001, the Chief of Women's Federation of Weishi County called me and asked if I had led reporters to Xingzhuang Township of the county to take photos of AIDS patients and those who died of AIDS. I said: "I do not know." Half an hour later, Wang Zhe, Vice-head of the Provincial Epidemic Prevention Center in charge of AIDS works, came to my home and again asked about reporters' taking photographs in Xingzhuang. I said I was busy having meetings recently and did not go out that month. An hour later, Li Chengxian, Vice-head of the Public Security Department of the province (head of the provincial working team in Weishi County), and Vice-county Head Lu also came.

Vice-county Head Lu said: "On the 21st and 22nd of this month, five reporters from *Beijing Legal Paper*, three males and two females (their leader called Lu Guang) came to Xingzhuang of Weishi County to take photos of patients and dead bodies. We want you to take the film back." He also said: "AIDS should not be frequently talked about. We are afraid that people might panic, local products will be refused by consumers, and the image of Henan will be affected."

Half an hour later, they left. Later, I was told that they enforced martial law in three counties and cities, but failed to find the reporters that night. Half a month later, I heard that the five reporters escaped back to Beijing that very night with the photos. In 2003, Lu Guang won first place at an international photo contest. Since then, Lu Guang's AIDS photos have been reprinted in several media publications at home and abroad, and he was placed under great pressure.

China Youth, October 31, 2005 --- Investigation in AIDS village by university students: AIDS has been threatening our loved ones beside us.

According to the latest official data, China had over one million AIDS virus carriers. Wang Longde, Vice-minister of the Ministry of Health, said on November 7, 2005, that only 5% of the carriers could be located and the other 95% had merged into the population.

According to the WHO's estimation based on an annual growth rate of 30%, by 2010, China will have ten million people infected with AIDS virus.

That means there will be one AIDS virus carrier among every 130 people.

In western countries, the AIDS virus spreads mainly through drug injection. In China, however, the biggest perpetrator may not be drug use or unsafe sexual activities, but group infection during blood trading under poor management.

II. Mobile blood trading is the source of spreading AIDS.

Blood trading is rampant in China. Many farmers sell blood from place to place. They may be in Henan or Hebei today, and in Shanxi or Shaanxi tomorrow, and in Shandong or Anhui the day after that. Each of these mobile blood sellers hold three to five "blood donor certificates" and they are professional blood sellers.

1. *Fujian Daily* reported that in 1997, Li Bencai and his wife Li Xiuhua left their hometown, Gongmin Town, Zizhong County in southwest Sichuan Province, and came to work at an electric appliance plant in Zhongshan City of Guangdong Province. At that time, Li Bencai could earn only 650 RMB per month and his wife earned even less. Living expenses in Guangdong were much higher than that in their hometown. No matter how frugal the couple was, they could not save money. Finally, Li Bencai thought of a way to earn money—by selling blood.

2. *China Youth* reported on December 1, 2005 that Lulou Village, Lixin County, Anhui Province, was composed of four natural villages, namely Luzhai, Lushuiyuan, Xizhuang, and Shiqiao. In the 1990s, because of a "blood disaster," 195 people in this village (with 1,256 villagers in total) were infected with AIDS. Statistics showed that 42% of the village population, or some 532 people in 324 families, once sold blood.

3. *Yangcheng Evening* reported that in late 1990s, some farmers in Shangluo District of Shaanxi Province suffered from a "strange disease" that could not be diagnosed for a long time. Later, repeated tests finally revealed that these farmers were infected with AIDS.

4. *Finance Magazine* in Shandong Province reported on May 2nd that the danger of AIDS infection by blood trading has not completely disappeared. At present, some underground blood stations still operate in Henan, Shandong, Shanxi, Anhui, and some other provinces. Large numbers of innocent farmers are still being misled by some propaganda. Knowing only benefits of blood selling and nothing about its drawbacks, they keep on selling blood.

From early 1990s to present, there have been six plasma collection stations in Shandong Province and they are located in Qihe, Zhangqiu, Xiajin, Yuncheng, Shenxian, and Yanggu, respectively. Some people witnessed that the latter three stations collected blood at night from 12:00 AM to 6:00 AM. Each blood seller sold 800 ml of blood each time and received 80 RMB.

One day in April 2005, someone witnessed a four-wheel lorry transporting some farmers who had just sold blood back to their homes. According to Yang, a blood seller, she sold blood four times a month, two times in Yanggu and two times in Shenxian. She earned over 300 RMB per month. She was 53 when she was interviewed. However, some regulations specified that people over 50 were not allowed to sell plasma and that the minimum time interval between two blood extractions should be two weeks. Yang had a fake ID card forged based on a borrowed residence booklet, and she just pasted her photo onto it.

5. *China Economic Times* reported on November 30, 2005, that the Health Department of Hebei Province announced that 80% of those infected with AIDS in Hebei Province were infected through blood contamination.

6. Reporters from the *China Economic Times* carried out three rounds of investigation in July and November of 2005 in some areas of Hebei Province, including Qiaoxi District, Qiaodong District, Julu County, Shahe City, Weixian County, Boxiang County, Xingtai County, Ningjin County, Guangzong County, Pingxiang County, and Renxian County, under the jurisdiction of Xingtai City, and Wu'an City, next to Shahe City (belonging to Handan District).

During the interview, almost all people infected with AIDS and their family members believed that they were "harmed" by the hospital. Their suffering today was caused by the hospitals transfusing contaminated blood into their bodies. It was an open "secret" that blood trading in 1990s infected many people with AIDS. Where does the contaminated blood flow? Up to now, 80% of all the AIDS patients I have seen were infected through blood transfusion. This was the beginning of the tragedy. How many people will be infected by blood containing the AIDS virus is a question yet to be answered.

III. Truth about AIDS spread

During a group consultation on April 7, 1996, I discovered a patient infected with AIDS due to a blood transfusion during a uterus operation. As she received blood from the blood bank, my keen sense told me that she would not be the only one infected with AIDS virus this way. It was strange, however, that all her family members, particularly her husband, did not catch AIDS. After knowing my concern, an official from the Provincial Health Department retorted: "You are good at making a scene. How can you be so lucky to see so many AIDS patients?" From then on, I began to doubt the past hearsay about AIDS spread by drug abuse and sexual promiscuity. Recently, I learned that, different from the situation in other countries, AIDS spread in China is mainly through "blood economy." However, government officials dare not bear responsibility, and they use every trick possible to cover up truth, safeguard their personal interests and the interests of their own group, and keep themselves in power. They have no concern about people's life and death. I had to investigate the spread of AIDS on my own.

I found many people infected with AIDS via blood or plasma transfusion. Take children patients for example: they cannot take drugs or be engaged in sexual activity. Their parents or other close acquaintances showed "negative" results during HIV-antibody testing. They received blood from AIDS patients and they were totally innocent.

Seeing economic growth, the current government regards China as a harmonious society and a rising power in the world. However, what I saw in the countryside were poor people badly in need of clothing and food. Violent cases happen from time to time in the whole country, and natural and manmade disasters occur one by one, especially the AIDS epidemic. AIDS will directly affect China's economic development and this is an undeniable fact. However, present-day Chinese have three characteristics: telling lies, practicing fraud, and faking.

In AIDS-related trade, there are numerous quacks (scam-artists) and fake medical practitioners. There are now even fake patients. Chen Fengyao, a self-proclaimed businessman from Taiwan, has fooled people around from northeast China to Henan. He spent 50,000 RMB on hiring each fake AIDS patient to speak in his favor. He claimed to have cured over 300 AIDS patients. Mo Yixian from Beijing introduced himself as a researcher from the Chinese Academy of Sciences and claimed to have cured over 100 AIDS patients. In fact, he is a swindler and used to sell pig feed. In his sixties, he deceived six girls from an AIDS epidemic area into becoming his concubines. A reporter disclosed his dirty tricks, and he put a bounty price of two million RMB on the reporter. Li Zhenxi from Henan called himself the first TCM doctor who could cure AIDS. In fact, he was a farmer in his hometown Gongyi City back in 1994. However, this quack was backed by corrupt officials. The wife of a department leader retorted to Li's critics on many websites: "If you do not know how to cure AIDS, you should let others try." Other quacks include Li Demin from Hubei, who called himself a "national treasure," and Sun Chuanzheng from Zhejiang, who claimed to have cured over 100 AIDS patients within three years. There are many, many other quacks and I cannot list them all here. More than one thousand such quacks have written to me or visited me. They bribed corrupt officials to be their backing and protective umbrella with the money they swindled out of AIDS patients. They also bought off some immoral reporters and media to do fake propaganda for them. These are great banes in the AIDS field, but no one bothers to investigate. On the contrary, many people side with the swindlers. This is a Chinese characteristic.

The patients infected with AIDS via blood transfusion were not only turned down when they tried to report the situation to the higher level or file a lawsuit, but even locked up by the authorities. An oral regulation specifies: the court won't accept the lawsuit concerning AIDS infection via blood transfusion. If you want to seek help from a lawyer, you will find that 50% of Chinese lawyers are politicians (they became lawyers because they have connection with officials in public security authority, procuratorate, or court) and 40% are money seekers who just muddle along. They speak gloriously but do nothing good. They are totally different from lawyers in other countries. I can give you four examples: Sun Xiaoyu, grandson of Sun Ya, and Jing Baobao, son of Fan Jiuzhi, two children infected with AIDS via blood transfusion after 2000, and husband of Wang Xiaoqiao, and Luo Fang herself—they each spent tens of thousands RMB on hiring lawyers.

I find what Chinese authority dreads most is that the true situation of AIDS epidemic will be made known to foreign leaders.

When former U.S. President Clinton came to give a speech at Tsinghua University, I was invited to attend the AIDS and SARS International Seminar held on November 10, 2003, and asked to give a speech in the afternoon. I arrived in Beijing on November 7th and settled in "Tsinghua Unisplendour International Center" at about 2:00 PM on November 9th. At 5:00 PM, Shi Ji, Party Secretary of my unit in charge of personnel, and Zhu Jinpin, Chief of the old cadre department, suddenly entered my room and said that they came to see me. Giving them no more chance to speak, I left my room and went to Beijing Normal University with the head of the Law Institute of Beijing Normal University. Before I left, they asked when I would be coming back. I said, "In the evening." That night, I stayed at Beijing Normal University and did not return to Unisplendour Hotel. At 8 AM the next morning, when I was to enter the meeting room, both Ji and Zhu were waiting for me at the entrance. They said, "Do not mistake us. We just want to have a word with you." I said: "That is unnecessary, I will attend this meeting. When I come back, it is up to you to take whatever measure you like." Then, a staff member of Tsinghua meeting organizing committee urged me to enter the meeting room. Ji and Zhu wanted to enter the room too, but were stopped by the meeting organizing committee. In the afternoon, foreign media made public the incident and asked: "Who said Gao Yaojie had personal freedom?" On November 12th, I returned to Zhengzhou. Now, six years have passed and no leader has ever talked to me about this incident.

In 2007, the United States awarded me the "Vital Voices" award, but the authority obstructed my going to the U.S. and put me under house arrest for half a month. Thanks to the efforts of Mrs. Hillary, the current U.S. Secretary of State, China finally let me go. However, they asked me to establish a foundation in the name of Gao Yaojie upon my arrival at the US. I refused to do so. I was still under surveillance even in the U.S. and they blocked my information channels, which angered Zeng Jinyan (wife of Hu Jia) to the point of tears.

After staying in the U.S. for over a month, many friends asked me to settle down in the U.S. They said, "For your safety, do not go back." My career was in China and there were many AIDS patients and orphans who needed me badly. I could not bear leaving them. So I returned. On the surface, the authority was good to me. They presented me with food and electric appliances. However, the reality was the opposite. They installed four surveillance cameras around my house and kept on monitoring my telephone, computer, and correspondence.

In February 2009, the U.S. Secretary of State Hillary visited China and requested to see me on February 22nd. The authorities agreed ostensibly. I arrived in Beijing on February 19th, and the following day, they dispatched Zhao Fenli, a long-retired vice-party committee secretary of the TCM College to Beijing too. They even used the police to try to stop me. Zhao thought I might stay in Zeng Jinyan's home. The national security personnel blocked Zeng's front door, prohibiting any one from going out or in. In fact, I did not stay in Zeng's home. After two days' futile searching, Zhao failed to find me. As for me, I was honored to be able to meet with the Secretary of State Hillary.

Since the 1980s, people began to classify AIDS as a venereal disease. Many believe that one won't catch AIDS so long as he does not take drugs, go whoring, or practice prostitution. In fact, most AIDS infections in China have been caused by the blood disaster. The spread of AIDS via sex and other channels only makes up a small proportion.

According to some relevant literature, the AIDS virus, or HIV, belongs to a human slow virus group, within a slow virus genus in the reverse virus family. According to HIV's gene and biological features, and the feature of the receptor used by HIV after its entry into the cell, HIV is divided into three types: gene type, biological type, and molecular type.

(1) **Gene type:** Based on gene difference, HIV is further divided into two types: HIV-1 and HIV-2. HIV-1 consists of M, O, and N subtype groups. M subtype group includes A1, A2, B, C, D, E, F1, F2, G, H, J, and K

subtypes. O subtype group and N subtype group are rare. HIV-2 is mainly seen in West Africa and West Europe. There are also a few reports from North America.

HIV-2 consists of A, B, C, D, E, F, and G subtypes. Its biological feature is similar to that of HIV-1, but with weaker virulence, longer course upon infection, and lighter symptoms. However, it is still incurable.

(2) **Biological type:** Based on the biological feature of HIV separation strain, there are the merging type and the non-merging type.

(3) **Molecular type:** Based on the feature of receptor using by HIV, there are X4 type and R5 type.

In central China, most AIDS virus infection cases are caused by B-subtype virus, which is rarely spread via sexual activity. In other countries, infection is mostly caused by subtype C-virus, which is easily spread via sexual activity.

We have seen a lot of cases in which a man or woman has AIDS, but his / her spouse and their child are not infected. This means that HIV infection follows certain scientific rules and that stereotyped propaganda will do nothing but cause panic.

There are over 3,000 villagers in a publicly-known AIDS village. In mid 1990s, over 1,500 villagers in this village sold blood. In early 2003, over 800 of them were confirmed to be suffering from AIDS. However, none of the villagers had used drugs. This reveals the true cause of the AIDS spread.

IV. AIDS takes away the youth and the middle-aged, dreadful life for the left-behind, old and young

In the late 1980s and early 1990s, AIDS had become a large-scale epidemic and been in focal spread. It was the "blood economy" that helped the AIDS virus to harm the ordinary people, mostly farmers. To improve their lives, build houses, get married, buy fertilizer, pay taxes, pay medical expenses, and pay tuition for their children, these farmers had to sell blood. To earn more, some even sold blood two or three times a day. They became weak and even fainted in the blood extraction process. Where did their blood flow? The contaminated blood was transfused into the patients under operation or critical patients. In this way, many innocent people were infected with AIDS and their infected number was higher than that of blood sellers. However, as they lived in different places, it was hard to locate them all.

Blood sellers began selling blood in groups, and villagers from over a dozen villages around a central key village became blood sellers at the same time. Around Wenlou Village are Houyang Village, Shaodian Village, Zhangyu Village, Wangying Village, Chenglao Village, and Zhangpolou Village. The AIDS epidemic in these villages were as serious as it was in the key village, and even more serious in some of these surrounding villages. The villagers caught AIDS, a long-course disease (may last over ten years), but they were illiterates who could neither write nor argue, and they found it hard to tell others about their suffering.

The families suffering from AIDS are now regretful about selling the blood. Who should be blamed? Whose sin is this? Who brought the suffering to these ordinary people? Up to 2009, not a single official has been held responsible for the "blood disaster".

AIDS brings about poverty and destroys people's lives. Suffering not only from illness, but from the coldness of society, AIDS patients are live a desperate life. Death is the unavoidable end for everybody, but for AIDS patients, death accompanies them every single day.

AIDS, the world plague, tortures the human body, causes economic loss, destroys family life, and kills countless people, mostly the young and the middle-aged. Left behind are the old and young. Children living in the shadow of AIDS are troubled by three major problems:

1. Survival: They lack food and clothing, especially in the bitterly cold winter. They have neither winter clothes nor shelter and nobody cares about them. Even so, some swindlers still cheat them into slavery or prostitution in other places in the name of "helping the orphans".

2. Education: Most AIDS orphans are school-aged. With no parent to guide them, they are easy led astray. Most orphans dislike learning and refuse to go to school even if you have paid tuition for them. Instead, they muddle around all day long, making trouble, fighting, stealing, and falling prey to villains. When they have turned bad, they end up damaging the social stability.

3. Psychology: Many children have had a contorted psychology. They find all things against them, refuse to communicate with others, and believe that other people have treated them unfairly. Some children even hate the society and form cliques to do whatever they like, regardless of whether it is legal or illegal. Some become robbers at a very early age. We have to worry about what they will become in the future.

In my opinion, the salvation of the orphans is only one side of the problem. The more urgent task is to stop the spread of the "blood disaster," which is the source of orphans. Otherwise, the "blood disaster" will kill more parents and create more orphans. I dare not imagine the outcome.

On April 30, 2001, I investigated a primary school in an AIDS-high prevalence area. Among the 100 students in the school, 29 were AIDS orphans. In January 2002, the headmaster of the school wrote to me, "Seven AIDS orphans graduated last year, but new orphans came. We now have 33 orphans in total and the number is still rising." Who can save these poor children?

On October 2, 2001, I went to another AIDS village and visited a dozen AIDS families. In this village, all children above the age of 12 had dropped out of school; the girls helped their families do chores and other labors while looking after the AIDS patients in their families. At only 14 or 15, some girls were "bought" by men in their 30s or 40s to be their wives. Worse still, some swindlers cheated the girls into going with them to work in other places, but the work turned out to be "prostitution". A "Boss Jin", who claimed to run a textile mill in Suzhou, hired six girls, aging from 16 to 19, from an AIDS village. When the girls arrived in Suzhou, they did not see the textile mill, but a large beauty parlor, and Boss Jin wanted them to serve the male customers. They knew what that meant and escaped in the dead of a night. Boys from the village ended up no better. Some 15 and 16-year-old boys do hard labors, unbearable even for adults, and many even became miners.

Since the autumn of 1996, I have written and printed 1.2 million copies of materials on AIDS prevention and handed them out throughout China. I have written seven books on AIDS prevention and distributed over 500,000 copies and published over one million copies of them in the country. The total expenses for doing these, including postal fees and trip expenses, totals over one million RMB, which was covered by my bonuses and remunerations as an author and my private savings. I have never received any donations. Why? Because I have been in a perilous position. Since 1999, I have found that the authorities were not friendly towards me.

V. What did I get from doing AIDS prevention and orphan-saving works?

In 2000, I was placed under surveillance and shadowing, and my telephone was monitored. They even forbade me to give science-popularization lectures in university, including those on AIDS knowledge. In 2001, I began helping AIDS patients and orphans. The authority forbade me to see reporters or investigate the AIDS epidemic in the country. They did not allow me to go abroad to receive awards. In 2003, the authority instigated a swindler to sue me. Although he lost the lawsuit, the authority kept its negative attitude against me. The dispute about the spreading channels of AIDS should be academic in nature. Helping AIDS patients is a good deed. The support for them, both in material and spirit, aims to grant them a better condition for survival. However, these loving actions were viewed by the government as the behavior of a dissident.

My family members have also been affected, including my younger sister and brother, and especially my three children. My son was thirteen when the Cultural Revolution began and was imprisoned for three years under the charge of "crime of counterrevolution". Even today, he is timid and is estranged from me. He is the best hostage with whom the Henan authority has punished me. Many people knew that on February 18, 2007, the day before my first visit to the US, the authority forced him to kneel down before me and 'kowtow' (bow) three times, asking me not to go to the US and receive the award. My youngest daughter, Guo Yanguang, immigrated to Canada with her husband as technical emigrants in 2000. Now, she is under the control of a rascal backed by the "National Security" personnel from Jiangmen of Guangdong Province. She is extremely hostile to me. The following is a letter she wrote to me (at 1:16 AM, October 20, 2009).

"[No theme]

From: "yanguang guo" <guoyanguang@yahoo.ca>

To: "Yao Jie Gao" <gaoyaojie2003@yahoo.com.cn>

You are on a path reviled by our countrymen. You can keep on making fuss this way. When you die, there won't be any relatives beside you. You will die in loneliness."

One day in 2007, a high-ranking official from the provincial government visited me. He said, "Secretary Xu (secretary of CPC Henan Provincial Committee) wants you to write a book entitled *Past and Present of AIDS in Henan*. You can first have a look around Wenlou Village of Shangcai County... The leaders say that we can organize a writing group and follow your instruction and use your signature only..."

I sensed something inside it and immediately refused the suggestion. Three days later, he called me again, but I still refused to write such a book. I knew why they treated me so well. They wanted me to say something untrue to cheat the others.

At the end of March 2009, a lady in the French Embassy called me: "France has decided to award you the Women's Human Rights Award." I told her that I was to receive an award in Shanghai in mid-April and we might talk about this then. She said OK. However, the award-giving ceremony in Shanghai was postponed for over a month.

On the morning of May 6, my telephone line was cut again by the authorities. At noon, a friend came to pick me up. She said: "You'd better leave. Trouble comes again." We had no time for lunch and immediately took a bus to Beijing. Three days later, I went to Langfang City. Over half a month later, I went to Sichuan. In early June, I went to Guangzhou and on June 12th, I settled down in Minglang Village on the suburb of Guangzhou, a quite remote area. I meant to stay there for a while, like I did last year to avoid the Olympic Games, and maybe two to three months later, I could go home. I wanted to deliver my manuscripts of three books to the publishing house. Otherwise, I would let the AIDS patients and their family members down, especially those who have died of AIDS.

I have dedicated myself to "AIDS prevention and orphan salvation" for over 13 years. Now, I can find no way out. The authority offers a reward of 500 RMB to the one who reports my whereabouts (50 RMB for others). They have tried all possible means to stop us (AIDS investigators and prevention supporters) from entering the AIDS villages. On March 14, 2003, Professor Gao Yanning, Du Cong and I went to Shuangmiao Village, an AIDS epidemic area, and we were nearly caught. The materials (books, clothes) I mailed to the poor epidemic areas were often confiscated by the authority. My daily life and activities have been restricted and my telephone and computer are constantly monitored. I am often shadowed and even put under house arrest. My personal freedom is restricted to such an extent that I cannot carry out my work.

In June, I learned that due to his investigation of the true number of the students who died during the Sichuan Earthquake, Mr. Tan Zuoren was arrested by Chinese authority under the accusation of "instigating to overthrow the state regime." Mr. Tan just wanted to help the vulnerable people, but he was met with much resistance and punishment. My work is similar to Mr. Tan's and is of wider scope, involves more people, lasts longer, and has greater impact. Seeing Mr. Tan's example, I have had to maintain sharp vigilance. I am not afraid of death. I just want to publish a book, telling the truth of the AIDS victims to our offspring; or, I will not be able to die in peace. That is why I left my home. I have cried too many times and my tears have soaked my pillow. I am over 80 already and my days in this world are numbered. Although I know that my present trip may end anytime and anywhere with my death, to tell the truth about China's AIDS epidemic, I had to do it.

In the past three to four years, I have realized that the AIDS epidemic is still serious in rural areas and blood stations have turned underground. **Now, there is a "plasma station" in Sunjiawan of Yunxian County, Shiyan City, Hubei Province. The operators organize over ten thousand women from the mountainous area to sell blood at 168 RMB per 600 ml (see *China Youth*, November 4, 2009).** There are many more undisclosed blood stations. So long as nobody speaks out, the officials can make a fortune and keep their grip on power. They have five methods to deal with those who speak out:

1. **Buying off with money, giving bribes, poverty relief, disaster compensation, and so on**

2. **Material temptation, presenting food, articles, furniture, electric appliances, even houses, automobiles, and so on**

3. **Giving honors, awards, promotion, party membership, and so on**

4. **Showing severe look, suppression, punishment, threatening, monitoring, house arrest, even making rumor, and so on**

5. **The last resort for those unyielding to the aforesaid methods: fabricating a charge to frame them and sending them to indoctrination through labor, criminal detention, and even imprisonment.**

These five methods are so effective that many who have dared speak out before have surrendered to temptation and threat. Some of them never speak out again. Some "able men" make an about-face turn and begin singing songs of praise. What a "peaceful and prosperous" society: AIDS under forceful control and the "blood disaster" being gone. They predict that in the future, AIDS will be spread mainly by drug abuse and sexual activity. Of course, the officials who have made a fortune by selling blood have also made excellent political achievements. Their personal interests and the interests of their group are maintained. No one cares about the well-being of the ordinary people.

The authority has many ways to put pressure on me. I give you an example. In early February 2007, three new visitors came to my Blog. Their names were "A Corner in the World", "Idiot, No Ordinary Idiot", and "Mouse with Double Eyelid." They had one thing in common: making irresponsible remarks. At one time, they said that my photos of AIDS patients were fakes fabricated by me. Another time, they said that I looked down upon sex workers (prostitutes). They made several dozen or even over a hundred comments a day. The most unbearable thing was that they made personal slurs against me, saying that I "was born to a poor family, was sold to a whorehouse at a very early age, and used to be a prostitute." They made such libelous comments for over ten days, and I doubted that others would ever know these were purposely made slanders. In fact, they were following the order of somebody behind the scenes. Later, I found out that one of them was a powerful woman in Henan. She had only a primary school education and was an active participant in the Cultural Revolution. She called herself an "excellent female cadre". To make herself beautiful, she had plastic surgery in South Korea and every month, she receives "creotoxin" injections. She claims to have received a Master's degree level education. In Henan, she is a big shot and nobody dares go against her.

Mine was an eminent family in Caoxian County of Shandong Province. In the end of the Qing Dynasty and at the beginning of the Republic of China, the Gao clan occupied over 3,000 mu of fields, which formed a separate village under the leadership of my father Gao Shengtan. His uncle, Li Wenzhai, was Chief of Kuomintang Party Committee in Shandong Province in the early 1930s and later a Kuomintang congressman. Li moved to Taiwan in 1948. My maternal grandfather, Xu Jiru, was a grand secretary of the Imperial Academy of the Qing Dynasty and an outstanding poet. Jia Hongchen, father of my second aunt, was a successful candidate in the imperial examinations at the provincial level in the Qing Dynasty. I was born in 1927 and received good Confucian education, which gave me an upright and outspoken character that defied brutal suppression.

On February 12, 1939, the second battalion of the Hebei-Henan-Shandong Border Area Detachment of the Eighth Route Army led by CPC occupied Gaoxinzhuang Village and took Gao Shengjun, Gao Shengtan, and another man away. They were tortured by the second battalion and several days later, the Gao family redeemed them back with 300,000 silver dollars (see Record of Caoxian County). Then, all properties of Gaoxinzhuang, on the surface and underground, were confiscated. After my entire family escaped to Kaifeng, our family properties were destroyed by fire.

This is my life story. In present China, you cannot totally believe what you read, because all know that China is a country of fakeness. I would like to back my story with facts.

I have several senior professional titles, including university professor and chief physician. However, some people may have doubts about this. In China, the higher the professional title, the more people make false claims. Some doctoral supervisors said: "Over 70% of the Doctors in China are fakes." In my case, however, I was a senior physician of the Department of Gynecology and Obstetrics. I have rescued many critical patients and solved lots of difficult cases through operations. I have given lectures to university students for over three decades. I'm not a party member. I have no governmental backing. What can I rely on if I have no real talent? How can I perform my duty without real ability and learning?

Several decades have passed and not a single official has been held responsible for the "blood disaster". If the officials are not wooing money and power, if the relevant departments are not indifferent, if the authorities care about people and do not cover up the truth—how can the AIDS epidemic be so serious?

○